Animal Fairy Tales

Sleeping Badger

written by Charlotte Guillain ☆ illustrated by Dawn Beacon

 Raintree

Chicago, Illinois

© 2014 Raintree
an imprint of Capstone Global Library, LLC
Chicago, Illinois

To contact Capstone Global Library please call 800-747-4992, or visit our web site
www.capstonepub.com

Edited by Daniel Nunn, Rebecca Rissman, and Catherine Veitch
Designed by Joanna Hinton-Malivoire
Original illustrations © Capstone Global Library, Ltd, 2014
Illustrated by Dawn Beacon
Production by Victoria Fitzgerald
Originated by Capstone Global Library, Ltd

Library of Congress Cataloging-in-Publication Data
Guillain, Charlotte.
  Sleeping Badger / Charlotte Guillain.
      pages cm—(Animal fairy tales)
  ISBN 978-1-4109-6115-0 (hb)—ISBN 978-1-4109-6122-8 (pb)—ISBN 978-1-4109-6135-8
  (big book) [1. Fairy tales. 2. Folklore—France.] I. Sleeping Beauty. English. II. Title.
  PZ8.G947Sl 2014
  398.2—dc23   2013011478
  [E]

Every effort has been made to contact copyright holders of material reproduced in
this book. Any omissions will be rectified in subsequent printings if notice is given to
the publisher.

Characters

Bella Badger

King and Queen

Fairy Godmothers

Wicked Wasp

Prince Snuffling

Once upon a time, a happy king and queen lived in a palace deep in the forest. Their happiness was complete when a baby princess was born. They named her Bella and held a big party to celebrate.

The king and queen invited three magic
butterflies to be their daughter's fairy
godmothers. Each godmother brought
a special gift for Princess Bella.

The first godmother gave the baby the gift of intelligence and fun. The second gave the gift of beauty and music. The third godmother was about to give her gift when a shadow fell over the room.

A wicked wasp flew in. She was mad that she had not been invited to the party.
"I put this baby under a spell," the wasp buzzed angrily. "She will be stung by a wasp and die before her 16th birthday."

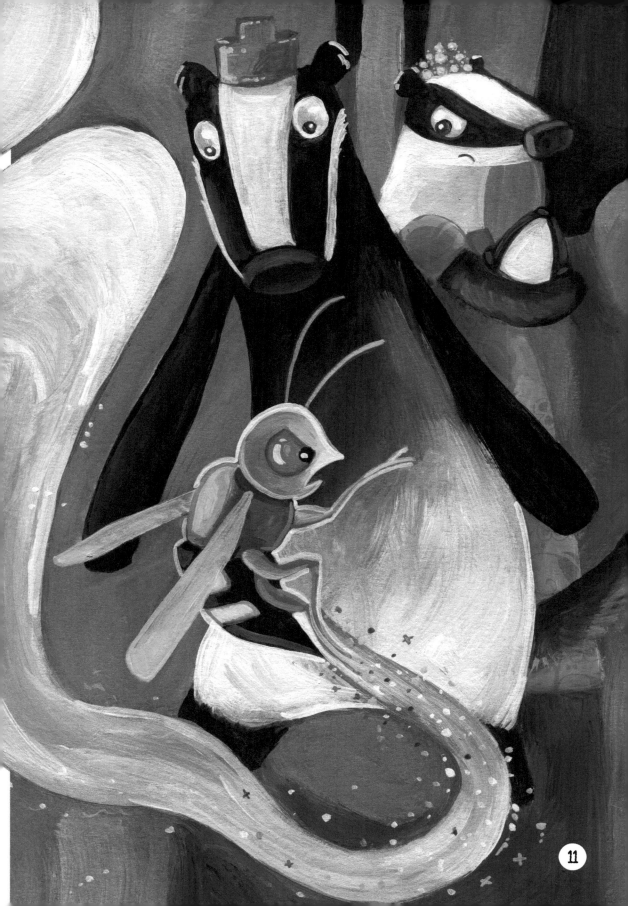

The wasp flew away, laughing. The last butterfly godmother thought quickly before she gave her gift to the baby.

"I cannot stop the wasp's spell," she said. "But if Bella is stung, she will not die. Instead she will sleep for 100 years and will only be woken up by a kiss from a prince."

The years passed and Bella grew up.
Everyone in the palace made sure that
no wasps ever came near her.

As her 16th birthday approached,
the king and queen hoped that Bella
might escape the wasp's spell.

But the day before her 16th birthday, Bella
heard a buzzing sound outside. She went
out to explore and saw a juicy apple.
She did not see the wasp hiding behind it.
As Bella reached out to take the apple, the
wasp stung her, and she fell asleep.

The king and queen were horrified.
They carried the sleeping Bella back
to her room. When the butterfly
godmothers saw how upset the king
and queen were, they magically put
everyone in the castle to sleep, too.

One hundred years passed and thorny
bushes grew around the sleeping palace.
One day, Prince Snuffling was passing
through the forest when he spotted the
palace behind the thick brambles. He cut
his way through and went inside, where
he found the sleeping princess.

Prince Snuffling thought Bella was beautiful! He gave her a kiss, and she began to wake up. Then everyone else in the palace began to stir. They were delighted to see Bella waking up.

It was not long before another party was held in the palace—for Bella and Prince Snuffling's wedding. And they all lived happily ever after.

 **The End**

Where does this story come from?

You've probably already heard the story that *Sleeping Badger* is based on—*Sleeping Beauty*. There are many different versions of this story. When people tell a story, they often make little changes to make it their own. How would you change this story?

The history of the story

Sleeping Beauty was first written by Charles Perrault in a collection of fairy tales in 1697. Charles Perrault collected popular folktales and created the first written fairy tales. Later the Brothers Grimm, from Germany, rewrote several of these stories.

In the original tale, a king and queen invite seven fairy godmothers to their daughter's christening. They begin to give the baby their gifts when they are interrupted by a wicked fairy who casts a spell on the princess, saying she will be pricked by a spindle and die. The last good fairy tries to counteract this spell by casting her own—the princess will instead fall asleep for 100 years and be woken up by a prince's kiss. Despite everyone's efforts, the princess is pricked by a spindle and falls asleep. The seventh fairy then puts everyone else asleep because they are so upset. She also makes thorns grow around the palace to protect the sleeping princess. After 100 years, a prince finds the palace and wakes up Sleeping Beauty. The spell is broken, and everyone lives happily ever after.